LEARNING TO LIVE
IN THE LOVE OF GOD

Learning to Live in the Love of God

Donald Pickerill

WHITAKER BOOKS
504 LAUREL DRIVE
MONROEVILLE, PA. 15146

Whitaker Books
504 Laurel Drive
Monroeville, Pennsylvania 15146

Cover design by Jerry Rosanski,
Scope Studios, Inc.

CONTENTS

FOREWARD

The studies presented in this book were first given at Desert Chapel in Palm Springs, California, during special Holy Week services. Having heard them delivered there and having felt their impact on my life, I encouraged Don Pickerill to put them into printed form so that the liberating message contained here could have wider circulation.

Rev. Don Pickerill has taught Bible courses for nearly twenty years at LIFE Bible College in Los Angeles, California. He received his formal training at such diverse institutions of learning as Kansas State Teacher's College, LIFE Bible College, Pasadena Nazarene College, Fuller Theological Seminary, the University of Judaism, and the University of Southern California. He has also pastored churches in La Crescenta and Los Angeles, California. Rev. Pickerill's ministry, both in teaching and pastoral work, has been characterized by a concern for people and a desire to see men made whole by the work of Christ in their lives.

These studies based on First John seem to me to be ideally suited for Christian growth groups and "prayer-and-share" groups in homes and churches. To help in this area, questions have been added after each chapter to encourage practical, personal discussion of the principles presented in the chapter.

Sam Middlebrook
LIFE Bible College
Los Angeles, California

LEARNING TO LIVE
IN THE LOVE OF GOD

Learning to Live in the Love of God

"In this the love of God was made manifest among us, that God sent his only Son into the world, so that we might live through him. In this is love, not that we loved God but that he loved us and sent his Son to be the expiation for our sins. Beloved, if God so loved us, we also ought to love one another."

1 John 4:9–11

One Thing in Common

We are all unique in many ways. We speak different languages; we are not the same age, sex, color, or race, nor do we share the same philosophy of life. But we all have one thing in common—life. And we want it with a capital L! We want life, and we want more of it (quality not just quantity), for life must turn qualitative before it becomes worthwhile. Some have answered the question, "Is life worth living?" in a desperate

11

way by doing away with it. So life demands more than just self-preservation; it includes also the preservation of a certain *kind* of self.

The Word of Life

This is a series about life. It is based on First John which was written to share the "word of life." John begins this letter by saying, "That which was from the beginning, which we have heard, which we have seen with our eyes, which we have looked upon and touched with our hands, concerning the word of life—the life was made manifest, and we saw it, and testify to it." The "word" of life, of course, is Jesus Christ. But it includes more than even the man Jesus. For Jesus is a personification of reality. The life was manifest in Him.

The word of life is the famous Greek phrase, *logos zoēs*. Among other things, *logos* was regarded as the essence of life, the very unifying principle of the universe. In Jesus, this life came to light, and He now makes it available in human experience. John goes on to describe the word of life in I John 1:3 as a common sharing, "a fellowship with us." And he goes on to say, "Our fellowship is with the Father and with His Son Jesus Christ." This life was manifest in Jesus, but it circulates in a wider society of the redeemed and accords with reality itself. Happily, the word of life holds forth the promise of a "complete joy" as John concludes in I John 1:4: "We are writing this that our joy may be complete." Let's take that same goal as our theme.

Love and Life

With an amazing simplicity John says in I John 1:5, "God is light," and in I John 4:8 he adds, "God is love." In summary, God is self-revealing and self-giving. This means that men can both know and experience the love of God. The formula is given in I John 4:9, "In this the love of God was made manifest among us, that God sent his only Son into the world, so that we might live through him." Notice the last three words, "live through him." Life through His love. That is the way. It is a love that John had fully experienced. As he reports in I John 1:1, John heard it, he saw it, and he touched it. The love of God reached John through Jesus, and the results showed up in life.

When Life Lacks Love

Life depends on love. Without love there is no fullness of life. The following letters are examples of what it means to live without experiencing authentic love. They are gratefully used by personal permission. A girl writes:

Our household was dominated by hostility. Mother against father, sister against sister, and sisters against parents. By the time I was eight years old, I had to be put on nerve pills. It seemed I could never please my mother. No matter how hard I tried to please her I couldn't. It was always—you can do better next time. Nothing was good enough.

I can remember getting so upset with myself for failing that I would actually hit my own head against the wall. I would do harm to myself and bite myself, and cuss myself out. That might be why even today I SEEM TO BE HAPPIEST WHEN I AM IN PAIN. A kind of self-punishment. I had a feeling that I was never loved, so I felt that I was no good.

When I was fifteen years old, my mom and dad broke up. The strain was so great I had a breakdown and developed ulcers. I know that I have no self love. I really don't like myself at all. I get very frustrated with myself and this ends up in depression. So I just hate me and the world. I have one of those "I'm-not-O.K.-and-you-are-not-O.K." attitudes. To this day I cannot tell my mother or father that I love

14

them; it just sticks in my throat. I wish I knew what to do. . .

A young man describes his experience this way:

I never found a milieu in my home where I could express my emotions and love. It is extremely difficult for me to express myself to anyone or give anything of myself to anyone (especially love). This causes me great emotional conflict, great interpersonal turmoil. It is due partly to the shallow relationship with my mother. She was always an authority; we had to do it her way or she was angry, sometimes venomous, giving us "dirty looks." She used to boast about me on the outside, but at home would tear me down. As a result, I can't help but feel that others do the same to me. (They may be pleasant and complimentary toward me in my presence, but behind me they probably speak lowly of me.)

I am strongly skeptical and cynical within myself and about others and myself. I have not learned to accept myself, and I don't think that others can accept me. My skepticism stems from the feeling that no one ever truly loved me or loves me, and I cannot conceive of God as the loving heavenly Father, but a God of just retribution and a punitive one. I find it difficult to believe that He loves me and so cannot accept myself as worth anything at all. I really despise myself and my existence; I suppose I am waiting for an existential "final experience" in which I will have authenticated myself. I live in *Angst* [German word for dread or anxiety] waiting for my life to become something meaningful. My efforts have proven futile; I can only wait.

What Is the Love of God?

The love John experienced is described this way in I John 4:10–11, "In this is love, not that we loved God but that He loved us and sent his Son to be the expiation for our sins. Beloved, if God so loved us, we ought also to love one another." Notice firstly, that the love of God is unmerited. He loved us when we did not love Him. "In this is love, not that we loved God but that He loved us . . ." God's love is unlimited and unmotivated, for the basis of His love is within Himself and does not depend upon the worth of the loved object. Here is a love, unlike limited love, with no strings attached.

Secondly, it is a demonstrated love. The love of God was made manifest in that "He loved us and sent his Son . . ." Genuine love is more than a gracious attitude; it also shows up in action. God's love is what He feels *plus* what He does. He sent His Son, and this means the fullness of Self-giving. The love of God is God giving *Himself* to us. And this is what we must have to be made whole. We

16

need to know of His love *toward* us, and we need to experience His love *in* us.

Thirdly, it is a practical love. God loves us at the point of our need, as sinners. As I John 4:10 concludes, "He loved us and sent His Son to be the expiation for our sins." If God *so* loved us, no wonder John exhorts us in I John 3:18, "Little children, let us not love in word or speech but in deed and in truth" (practically and really).

What is the love of God like? It is a sacrificial self-giving. It is God giving Himself, His life, to us. It is a gracious acceptance of those who do not love in return, and it positively acts in response to the deepest human need. Once this liberating truth grips our consciousness, it breaks all bonds of inner condemnation and fear.

God's Love at Work in Our Lives

Gods loves us. He loves us greatly; He loves us graciously; He loves us genuinely. Say those words to yourself, "God loves me." Make it personal. It can change your life and set you free. A lady shares in the following letter what the love of God did for her in a personal and practical way:

I know my parents loved me, but for some reason in my own mind I felt they rejected me. I never

17

felt that I ever pleased them, making them proud as parents. In fact, much of the time I felt like they were probably ashamed of me. I realize now that this was not their fault, but I had all these thoughts about myself because of my own self-rejection and hate.

But the person that made the biggest impression on my life was my sister. We were abnormally close. I just wrapped myself up in her because she was all I ever wanted to be. I began to lose, or maybe I just never found, my own identity. I withdrew from everyone—in fact I never talked unless someone asked me a question. I felt so inferior. I lived in constant self-condemnation. I carried an awful sense of fear about everything and everyone. If anyone ever had a meaningless existence, it was I.

By the time I was in junior high, I would go into the restroom at lunch time and wait for the bell, because I didn't know if anyone would let me sit with them. (This continued through high school.) I *thought* nobody liked me; I was ugly and dumb, and the less people had to be with me the better they would like it.

It wasn't until my third year of college that the break through came for which I had been searching so desperately. I began to learn to accept God's love for me, and then to love myself and accept the love others had for me but I had never been able to receive. It has changed my life. I began to come out of my shell. I saw the talents and good qualities of my life for the first time. I gained a confidence

I never had before. I have an authority of who I am and don't have to cower any more. Through the freedom the Lord has given, the self-condemnation is no longer a hang-up and I can truly accept myself. It has opened a new "Me" to me and makes me aware of the uniqueness and beauty of each individual God has made.

Seemingly it takes a poet to tell the heart of things. Notice the beautiful words of the last stanza of "The Love of God."

> Could we with ink the ocean fill,
> And were the skies of parchment made,
> Were every stalk on earth a quill,
> And every man a scribe by trade;
> To write the love of God above,
> Would drain the ocean dry;
> Nor could the scroll contain the whole,
> Tho' stretched from sky to sky.

PRAYER

Life with a capital "L"? Lord, is that really possible for me? Can you show me that kind of Life that is filled with Love, Your own Love for me? . . . Oh, but You already did. You showed me Life and Love when You showed me Jesus. Thank You, Father; I receive it gratefully.

Amen.

THINKING IT OVER . . .

1. Are you completely happy with your life as it is now? If you could add one element to your life, what would it be?
2. "Life depends on love." Do you feel that your life lacks love?
3. The young man quoted in this chapter says he had the feeling that "no one ever truly loved me or loves me." Think of a time when someone expressed love toward you. Were you able to believe you could be loved?
4. "IN THIS IS LOVE, NOT THAT WE LOVED GOD BUT THAT HE LOVED US . . ." Can you really believe that God loves you as you are, "with no strings attached?"
5. As the author suggests, say these words to yourself, "God loves me." Does your heart agree with what your lips are saying?

Reshaping Your Self-Image

"We are God's children now,"   I John 3:2

Who Am I?

Psychologist Carl Rogers claims that every human being is engaged in a lifelong process of trying to protect, maintain, and enhance his self-image. The self-image is obviously a major life factor. Though not exactly the same thing as the self, it can drastically shape the self. It makes a big difference, for example, how we answer the question, "Who am I?" The self-image is a construct of what we understand ourselves to be. It comes from many sources, being mediated to us mostly out of our past and from our parents. The problem with the self-image is that it may or may not accord with the facts. For instance, some beautiful people think they are ugly; and average, even superior people, often feel inferior.

A False Self-Image

A false self-image can be crippling. Listen as a man describes how he was devastated by a supposed superior self-image:

As a child, I was overly pampered and protected. Here is where I first got the notion that I was something extra special. But in grammar school I was treated like everyone else and had to depend upon myself for the first time. Being equal to others at school clashed violently with home life where I was a much cherished and unique jewel. This was disastrous to my self-image. I did not excel in sports. I did not excel in academics. I even bombed out socially.

By the time I reached high school, I was really disillusioned. My life became a paradox of trying to prove that I really was the superchild of my early childhood without putting forth a show of all-out effort. I took on the look of complete apathy. But at the same time, I was a perfectionist. As the typical perfectionist, I say if something is worth doing, it is worth doing perfectly.

This attitude has brought many anxieties and frustrations into my life. Every school assignment is a personal battle. Any grade less than an "A" is looked upon as failure. I put things off, I tell myself, until such time as I can give them my undivided attention. Soon it is too late to devote the time required for perfection. Finally it is never done. The sick feeling of failure settles over me. My stomach feels like a Westinghouse double load washing machine in full operation. Unhappily, I am the epitomy of frustrated perfectionists.

But I am coming to understand through the help of God that I am prone to fall short of the mark. This is the reason Jesus died for me, i.e., so that I wouldn't, because of my failures, live a life of guilt and defeat. Now that I am a Christian I am learning that the Lord doesn't damn me for past performances. I am not perfect. My Heavenly Father, however, accepts me as I am. I am loved and accepted because of *my standing as a son.*

Our True Self-Image

According to John, man's true self-image stems from his relationship with God. He writes in I John 3:2, "We are God's children now." Think of the dignity and value this adds to our self-definition, for man made in the "image and likeness of God" is certainly a far cry from a "naked ape." Our sense of sonship is overwhelming evidence of the love of God. John goes on to explain in I John 3:1, "See what love the Father has given us, that we should be called the children of God;

and so we are." So we are God's sons now, not in name only, but in fact. Who am I? I am a child of God. I am a being of infinite worth made in the image of God, loved with an everlasting love, destined for an eternal glory.

No Longer But Not Yet

Someone said that Christians are a people who are "no longer" but "not yet." We are no longer what we were, and we are not yet what we shall be. To use John's words in I John 3:2, "it does not yet appear what we shall be." This means that the full benefits and implications of our sonship have not yet been revealed. The world is "waiting for the manifestation of the sons of God," as Paul says in Romans 8:19. We *are* sons, right now, but we are not "manifested." This will not happen until Jesus comes back.

In the meantime we must go on contending with life in an unredeemed world. John does not mince words at this point as he describes the sin struggle in I John 1:10 and I John 2:1: "If we say we have not sinned, we make him a liar, and his word is not in us. My little children, I am writing this to you so that you may not sin; but if anyone does sin, we have an advocate with the Father, Jesus Christ the righteous."

A Heavenly Father

John sounds like a loving elderly parent calling his readers, "My little children." Parents challenge their children to perfection but know all the while that they are imperfect. The same is true of our Heavenly Father. He urges us to reach for the stars, but He never rejects us for the dust on our feet. God is not an impossible parent. He is not picky and oppressive. As James 1:5 puts it, "God upbraideth not." It means He does not scold or nag with an underlying attitude of rejection. In today's language, He does not put us down; on the contrary, He loves us and freely accepts us as imperfect sons. In the 103rd Psalm, David sang about God's love for sinful sons:

"The Lord is merciful and gracious,
  slow to anger and abounding in steadfast love.
He will not always chide,
  nor will he keep his anger forever.
He does not deal with us according to our sins,
  nor requite us according to our iniquities.

27

For as the heavens are high above the earth,
   so great is his steadfast love toward those who
   fear him;
As far as the east is from the west,
   so far does he remove our transgressions from
   us.
As a father pities his children,
   so the Lord pities those who fear him.
For he knows our frame;
   he remembers that we are dust."

A Process-People

We are sons of God now, but we are a people
in a process, sons in the making. This truth must
go into the construct of our Christian self-image,
or we will fall prey to the twin problems of self-
condemnation or self-righteousness. Our standing
is perfect; our state is imperfect. Consequently,
the standard whereby we measure our acceptabil-
ity must be God's, not ours. We are too prone to
subjectivity and bondage to our "inner child of
the past." We simply cannot trust any human
judgment in this matter, certainly not our own
feelings or conscience. John counters this in I John
3:20, "If our heart condemn us, God is greater
than our heart."

The conclusion is: God accepts us so we can accept ourselves. Our self-image is sons-in-the-making. This is a true self-image. It fits the facts of our experience and accords with the Biblical account. It is, incidentally, life's greatest challenge and yet it is not defeating, for it is gracious. Sons, but sons-in-the-making, that's who we are. It keeps us hopeful and humble, all at the same time.

Plastic Surgery

Two things are needed to reshape a self-image: a definition plus a dynamic. We need to know who we are and we need an inner power to become what we are. This is why life needs light and love. The Frenchman who coined the famous phrase, "Everyday in every way I am getting better and better," reportedly committed suicide. It takes more than words and mere outward changes. Plastic surgeon, Maxwell Maltz, has confirmed this in one of his best-selling books. He tells of some patients with improved physical features who become happier. Others, however, react in a puzzling way. They would look into a mirror and freeze into indifference. Their outer appearance had changed, but they could not accept or enjoy it. In his opinion, the physical change meant nothing because there was no change on the inside.

Spiritual Surgery

A shortened nose, a finely chiseled chin, or a new hair-do may help, but we really need a more radical type of change to reshape our self-image. In order to sustain a permanent change, we need a spiritual surgery. Various illustrations are used in I John to describe the dynamic power of this inner renewal. It is likened to a light that shows us where we are going (I John 2:11), anointing that brings knowledge (I John 2:20), a divine birth making us overcomers (I John 2:29 and I John 5:4), and an impartation of God's nature (I John 3:9). In summary, it is an indwelling of Jesus through the Holy Spirit as He shows Himself in a life of love.

A life indwelt by the Holy Spirit may sound mystical, but it is really very practical. Ask the average person what kind of ideal characteristics he wishes he possessed. Most would include such things as: love, joy, peace, patience, kindness, goodness, faithfulness, gentleness, and self-control. This enviable list happens to be, of course, a quotation of the nine-fold fruit of the Spirit named in Galatians 5:22–23. The indwelling of the Holy Spirit should not make us odd or spooky people. His work is to normalize us. For the most spiritual man is the most natural man. God wants to affirm life not negate it, open our eyes not close them. Jesus Christ was the most natural, winsome, wholesome man who ever lived. And through His indwelling He wants to reproduce that kind of life in us.

We cannot change ourselves by self effort alone. We need a Savior. And the Savior must enable us to live in love. All these necessary elements are found in I John 4:13–16: "By this we know that we abide in him and he in us, because he has given us of his own Spirit. And we have seen and testify that the Father has sent his Son as the Savior of the world. Whoever confesses that Jesus is the Son of God, God abides in him, and he in God. So we know and believe the love God has for us. God is love, and he who abides in love abides in God, and God abides in him."

The spiritual surgery may seem imperceptible at first, but it is going on in the inner man, in the subconscious life. Even with the new birth, we still struggle with sin and we fall short. But we will not ultimately fail, as John confidently asserts in I John 4:4, "Little children, you are of

God, and have overcome them; for he who is in you is greater than he who is in the world." Our part is to receive Jesus Christ as our Savior, turn our lives over to His Lordship, and let Him begin His transforming work as He reshapes not only our self-image but our real selves.

A Testimony of Transformation

In the following testimony, a Christian nurse tells how the love of Christ is reshaping her self-image:

As I sit here on my bed and painfully think of expressing my inner feelings concerning my self-image, I see a great change in my views of late. To give you a true picture I feel I must relate the "me" before the transition and the "me" now. When I was a child growing up, I was always over-weight. I was a compulsive eater with a doting grandmother who thought "chubby" children were healthier. When I was ten years old, my parents divorced. I got ulcers and had such emotional problems that I was unable even to attend school for four years.

My obesity resulted in great feelings of inferiority, self-consciousness, and a feeling of complete unacceptance around peers. I had no close friends, and as soon as school was over, I would walk thirteen blocks to a place where my mother worked. My inner self was seething like a raging sea.

The "me" now: My self-image is daily responding to God's healing process. I no longer have the terrible inferior feelings; whenever things start to arise, I remind myself that I am loved for who I am. My human need for a fulfilling experience is being fulfilled and as a result, my abnormal feelings are being dissolved by God's processes. I am becoming what Christ designed me to be. I am sufficient in Him. God is completely healing me physically and emotionally.

PRAYER

A CHILD OF GOD! What a beautiful ring that expression leaves in my ears, Father. Why did it take me so long to realize that those words apply to me? You tried to tell me over and over again. You called me "Son" repeatedly, and my Older Brother kept leading me into Your presence and telling me of my privileges as Your son. But now I see it: A CHILD OF GOD! All glory be to the Father.

Amen.

THINKING IT OVER . . .

1. List three words which you feel describe you best:

   _____

   _____

   _____

2. List three words which you think your friends would use to describe you:

   _____

   _____

   _____

3. The nurse mentioned in this chapter said, "I am becoming what Christ designed me to be." What has Christ designed you to be? Is that design becoming a reality in your life?

4. "We are God's children now," I John 3:2. What does this statement tell you about your true self?

5. How does God provide for your life since you are one of His children?

Living Victoriously

>>><<<

"Whatever is born of God overcomes the world; and this is the victory that overcomes the world, our faith,"
I John 5:4

A Doctrinal Danger

First John was written against a doctrine known as Docetism. It was a tenet of a widespread philosophico-religious movement called Gnosticism, which was characterized by the central doctrine that deliverance comes through knowledge, *gnosis,* the possession of which saved the initiates from the clutch of matter. The word "Docetism" is merely a Greek term meaning "to appear" or "to seem." It has been nicknamed the doctrine of "seemism," for the so-called Christian Gnostics claimed that God only seemed to be present in the man Jesus. According to them, it was quite impossible for this life to merge with eternal life.

On the contrary, the goal of life was to escape life. Through knowledge man was to remove himself as far as possible from matter. This meant that life consisted of two separate and distinct parts: on the one hand was the realm of God, the human soul, and eternal life; while on the other hand was the realm of Satan, the human body, and this life.

Since Jesus had a human body, He could not, of course, have been the incarnate Son of God. They reasoned that the "Christ" was a spiritual emanation from God—but separate from the man Jesus—that came on Jesus at His baptism but left Him before His death on the cross. This helps explain the strange passage in I John 4:6 which says, "This is he who came by water and blood, Jesus Christ, not with water [baptism] only, but with water and the blood [the cross]." All sorts of strange doctrines, especially about sin, came out of these conclusions. Since the body and the soul were altogether different realities, sins done in the flesh were not significant. It obviously follows that the Gnostics alone possessed this supposed superior knowledge without which others could not be emancipated. John wastes no time on them when he reminds his readers, "you have no need that any one [of these false teachers] teach you," (I John 2:27).

Religion and Reality

A subtle danger exists in separating religion from reality, this life from eternal life. In I John, the main proof that the two can be one is the person of Jesus, for eternal life was in Him. According to I John 4:2, the chief Christian confession is that Jesus Christ is the Son of God: "Every spirit that confesses that Jesus Christ has come in the flesh is of God." The key connection is "Christ . . . in the flesh." This single truth has enough spiritual dynamite to explode much of the world's religions, including any escapist notion in Christian circles. Eternal life is "down here" as well as "out there."

The goal of life is to enter into life. Jesus came to normalize existence by enabling us to live in reality, not run from it. The resurrection of the body with an endless existence is a blessed hope. But it is the resurrection of *the body*, not the immortality of the soul which we anticipate. Separating the soul from the body is pagan doctrine, brought in mostly by Greek philosophy. Jesus came to raise this life to its highest power and then at the end to raise the body from the dead. Abundant life merely becomes eternal life; the two remain inseparable. John put it in a very practical way in I John 3:6: "He who abides in him ought to walk in the same way he walked." In Christ the "ought" can become the "is."

Becoming an Overcomer

One of the most intriguing passages in I John is what appears to be a form of poetry in 2:12–14. It is made up of two sequences, each with a triple address to "children, fathers, and young men." Quite likely, it is a stylistic device emphasizing different Christian experiences: fathers (those old in the faith) are credited with knowledge; young men (those growing in the faith) are identified with strength; and the children (new converts) are experiencing forgiveness of sins and dependence on God the Father. All these qualities and promises, of course, apply to every believer. The significant thing is that the subject of sin, knowledge, and victorious living are joined together. This seems to imply that an overcomer must intelligently face sin. Let's follow John's lead and see what he says about the subject.

I. JOHN MAKES A DISTINCTION BETWEEN VARIOUS LEVELS OF SIN.

John did not fall into the error of the Gnostics who separated the body from the soul and associated sin with matter. But he does draw valid distinctions between various forms of wrongdoing. His valuable words in I John 5:16–17 are:

"If any one sees his brother committing what is not a mortal sin, he will ask, and God will give him life for those whose sin is not mortal. There is a sin which is mortal; I do not say that one is to pray for that. All wrongdoing is sin, but there is sin which is not mortal."

The truth that all sin is not the same is very important, for it enables us to distinguish various levels of wrongdoing. For example, people may have all kinds of emotional weaknesses and maladjusted tendencies which need correcting but do not involve real guilt. The basis for John's distinction between sins probably goes back to the Old Testament. In Numbers 15:27, 28, 30, Moses separated "sins with a high hand" and "error done unwittingly":

"If a person sins unwittingly he shall offer a female goat a year old for a sin offering. And the priest shall make atonement before the Lord for the person who commits an error, when he sins unwittingly, to make atonement for him; and he shall be forgiven . . . But the person who does anything with a high hand, whether he is a native or a sojourner, reviles the Lord, and that person shall be cut off from among his people."

Maladjusted Impulses

W. Curry Mavis has written an enlightening study entitled "Understanding Maladjustive Impulses." He claims that there are two interior sources that provide urges to wrongdoing. Firstly, there are the natural and inborn tendencies to sin which theologians have termed innate sin. Secondly, there are the repressed complexes and maladjustive impulses which have been acquired in life experiences. These maladjustive impulses are centers of psychic energy that have been built up through frustrating experiences in life. They come from what we might call the consequences of sin. Psychologically they are "hangups." Hangups come to us because we are born into an imperfect world. We do not freely choose them; they happen to us. So we have two tendencies in our personality: the rebellious drive to run our own lives in a willful and wrong way, plus the "elemental spirit" or "inner child of the past" shaped partly by experiences beyond our conscious control.

Conversion

Contrary to some expectations, conversion does not cleanse away our maladjusted impulses all at once. Personality growth is a process; maturity takes time. The gift of life is instantaneous; acquiring health may be gradual. The psychologically immature adult is not suddenly made mature by any great religious experience, for the Holy Spirit is not some Divine magic that by-passes all moral and normal growth processes. Many emotional deposits left over from our childhood handicap our true self. These distinctions must be made or we may have chronic guilt feelings and never learn to live in the love of God. Here is an example from a dedicated Christian who tells of his personal struggle:

One of the most prominent fears I exhibit is fear of people. I think the historical roots arise from a seventh grade teacher who was determined to humiliate me. He stood me up in front of the class and ridiculed and made fun of me. From that time on, I had very little confidence.

I was also influenced by the poor advice of my father who said, "You don't have to love the world to live in it." He told me a story of how he made one of his best friends in high school by first getting into a fist-fight with him. I subconsciously decided to do the same and became involved in several fights during my high school years. People became a threat to me because I thought that I had to conquer them to be their friend—or at least prove to them I was not afraid.

During my teenage years, I had very few friends. I did not get along with the majority of students, but I was especially unpopular with the "in" crowd.

I blamed my dislike for them and their dislike for me upon their basic immaturity. My parents aided me in building this defense mechanism by consistently degrading the "Dumb Frenchmen," who were the majority of the population in the town. My father affirmed that the reason I was not liked was because we had the wrong name, an Irish one.

Even today, my *spontaneous* first reaction is to shift the blame somewhere else. Some time ago, a woman who assists me in correction of technical problems on electronic equipment received an electrical shock because I had failed to disconnect the unit from the power line. My first reaction was, "You should keep your hands out of there!" I had immediately wanted to shift the blame back on her. After a few minutes, I realized what I had done and apologized for not disconnecting the power before directing her to work on the equipment.

II. JOHN SAYS TO ASSUME FULL RESPONSIBILITY FOR REAL SIN AND OPENLY FACE IT.

The famous confession formula, "No Denial," found in I John 1:8–9, reads, "If we say we have no sin we deceive ourselves, and the truth is not in us. If we confess our sins, he is faithful and just, and will forgive our sins and cleanse us from all unrighteousness." A "mortal" sin would have

44

to be more than some specific immoral conduct, for I John 1:7 promises, "If we walk in the light . . . the blood of Jesus cleanses from all sin." This suggests that the deadly sin is "not walking in the light," or denying that we have sin. In this case, it is the refusal to take the antidote and not the poison that kills. To put it in a clumsy way: the problem is not the problem, the problem is the problem plus a denial of the problem. Rather than our sin, it is a rejection of the Savior that is fatal. Man was not made for deception. The denial of a problem leads on to a self-made prison. Rugged honesty, courageous sincerity, candid confession—these are the keys to victorious living. There are no substitutes.

Acceptance

If we confess our sins, we receive a forgiveness which is rooted in the very nature of God who is faithful and just. To be forgiven means to be accepted, and to be accepted is to be victorious. Dr. C. G. Jung, Swiss psychiatrist, claims that acceptance is the epitome of the whole outlook on life:

The acceptance of oneself is the essence of the whole moral problem and the epitome of the whole

outlook upon life. That I feed the hungry, that I forgive the insult, that I love my enemy in the name of Christ—all these are undoubtedly great virtues. But if I should discover that the least among them all, the poorest of all the beggars, the most impudent of all the offenders, the very enemy himself—is *myself*—what then? As a rule the Christian attitude is reversed; there is no longer any question of love or long suffering; we say to the brother within us, "Raca," and condemn and rage against ourselves. We hide it from the world; we refuse ever having met this least among the lowly in ourselves. Had it been God Himself who drew near us in this despicable form, we should have denied Him a thousand times before a single cock had crowed. For man to accept himself in all his wretchedness is the hardest of tasks, and one which is almost impossible to fulfill.

A Personal Testimony

As we learn to live in the love of God, we find no need to hide from our hangups or our sins. Our acceptance from Him gives us the freedom for self-acceptance. A young lady who calls herself "Miss Perfectionist" tells how a victorious peace came to her through Jesus:

I find that I repress my true feelings. I have a tendency to run away from a problem, rather than trying to solve it. All my life, I felt that people would

46

not accept me if they knew my father was a heavy drinker. Consequently, this was the beginning of *hiding* my deepest concern from other people, even my closest friends. I felt I always had to appear happy and vivacious, always helping others, always looking like I just came from the hairdresser's. I was known as "Miss Perfectionist" and I felt I had to live up to this image regardless of the cost. The cost was great. I came very close to a nervous breakdown; no longer could I sleep at night.

The greatest lesson I believe I have learned since I have been a Christian is that I must be my real self, and that I must not repress my feelings. I realize now that I am just as important to God as anyone else. Even though I came from a home which was not a Christian one, that does not make God love me less than someone who came from a Christian home.

I have also come to realize that I do not have to work to be accepted. I just have to be myself. I used to run mentally through conversations that I might get involved in during an evening, just so I would have the right words to say. Because of this, I was a little "up-tight" all the time. But now I have accepted myself; therefore, I realize that other people accept me as well. Now I just let the Holy Spirit guide me. It is very easy this way—allowing God to use me. I am His child and His servant. I have such a peace in my life now. *I am resting in Jesus.*

PRAYER

Lord, I still feel that old tendency to run and hide when I have done wrong, to separate myself from You, or to deny that I have sinned. And I know better. You have been teaching me that the only way to have sin forgiven is to confess it. I believe, Lord, help my unbelief. Through Jesus my Savior.

Amen.

THINKING IT OVER . . .

1. The author states that we have two tendencies to wrongdoing in our personalities. Give an example of each one of those in your life.

   (1) "The rebellious drive to run our own lives in a willful and wrong way"

   _____

   _____

   (2) "The elemental spirit or inner child of the past shaped partly by experiences beyond our conscious control"

   _____

   _____

2. The Christian in this chapter telling of his personal struggle says: "My spontaneous first reaction is to shift the blame somewhere else." Is this true of you? How does this thwart victorious living?

3. What is the connection between forgiveness and acceptance?

Facing Life with Freedom and Confidence

"In this is love perfected with us, that we may have confidence for the day of judgment, because as he is so are we in this world. There is no fear in love, but perfect love casts out fear. For fear has to do with punishment, and he who fears is not perfected in love."   I John 4:17–18

Living Naturally

It is a wonderful thing to live naturally, in a free and spontaneous way. We need no convincing that life ought to be lived in freedom and confidence. The bondage of timidity and fear is self-evident. A student describes the torment of "being bound and tied up on the inside."

My self image is like a maze; I am full of passageways and dead ends. Almost all my life, I have been worried over what people are thinking of me. "Do

I smell okay?" "Is my hair combed neatly?" "Are my clothes clean and do they smell clean?" And on and on and on. At times I get so mad at myself because it hinders me from being natural. I cannot be myself in a natural, spontaneous way. It is getting to the point where I am literally feeling bound by this attitude. I can remember times when I really wanted to enter into fellowship with people, enjoy their company, have fun with them, talk with them; but I have not done so because I feel bound and tied up inside. I cannot enjoy life because I am afraid of what people think of me. Spontaneity is foreign to me because of this fear.

The urge in me to run is very great. In my dreams, I am always on the run either from a group of men like an army, or someone in authority. The dreams always end whenever I get cornered and find no way out and the ones looking for me find me. I wake up breathing very fast, perspiring, and feeling scared. I always get the feeling I am running and hiding from someone or something.

I get very nervous whenever I ask a question in class. My whole insides literally shake. One day in class Rev. Pickerill pointed out that many times our physical bodies experience sickness because of what we are mentally. Instantly, I thought of the migraine headaches that I had had for eleven years. I knew that there was nothing organically wrong with me; medical tests have proven this. I raised my hand to ask the question about my headaches. Immediately

I felt scared, flushed, shaky, perspiring, and very hot. I felt every eye in the class on me when I asked my question. My hand started twitching, my foot began tapping, and my leg began to swing back and forth at a moderate pace. I felt very emotional. Then the final response my body gave was my throat drying up and I could hardly speak.

I usually take the most insignificant little thing that might have happened and think on it until it is a major catastrophe. A very good example of this "mind-building" is being jealous of my wife. To me, being jealous is one of the most childish and immature motives a person can have. And yet no matter how much I despise it, I experience jealousy time and time again. To begin with, my jealousy is of the worst kind—unfounded, with no basis, no real reason for being jealous. My wife can have a simple conversation with someone and immediately my mind will make an "affair" out of it. But one day I know I'll be rid of this torment through God's help.

According to I John 4:17, freedom and confidence is one of the effects of living in the love of God. "In this is love perfected with us, that we may have confidence . . ." John uses the word "confidence" four times in this letter: I John 2:28; 3:21; 4:17; and 5:14. It is described as the opposite of "shrinking in shame" in I John 2:28. And in I John 3:21, it is the opposite of condemnation:

"If our hearts do not condemn us, we have confidence." It comes from a Greek word, *parrēsia,* which has the root idea of something that flows or moves freely. Throughout the New Testament, it is translated by such English words as: *openly, plainly, boldly,* or the nouns *confidence* and *freedom.* The word was especially connected with speech, almost like our celebrated English idea of "freedom of speech." John applies it to our speech before God in prayer in I John 5:14: "This is the confidence which we have in him, that if we ask anything according to his will he hears us." So we are talking about a life that can be transparently open, with the ability to speak boldly and an inner freedom to face the future with confidence and poise. John gives a two-fold formula for this liberating freedom: (1) if our heart is not under condemnation, I John 2:21, and (2) if we have been perfected in the love of God, I John 4:17.

Confidence and Condemnation

Confidence and condemnation are directly connected, for an uneasy conscience is a powerful negative force in human life. Indeed, "guilt makes cowards of us all," or as John says, we "shrink in shame." We may disguise it or even consciously be unaware of it, but an inner judgment against the self is devastating. Under condemnation, a person loses confidence and freedom. In the following letter a young wife shares the type of torment caused by guilt:

I've always thought of myself as a "clod." As a child, I was always the tallest in my class; my ski-jump nose was a point of ridicule. I was perpetually overweight and terribly clumsy. I am constantly striving for self-satisfaction.

I'm in a vicious circle. I'm always combating an inner self-image of irresponsibility, impulsiveness, over-verbalization, and basic guilt for *everything* I do. It's so frustrating to live this way because everything I'm involved in or say, no matter how simple, becomes a point of condemnation.

I'm constantly striving to fulfill this inner need of satisfaction, and it drives me to exhaustion. I'm never content with the state I'm in. It's strange, the only time I'm not in this rut is when I finally collapse and I'm sick in bed. I've found myself enjoying illness because it's the only place of relaxation. Unfortunately, my guilt feelings won't let me enjoy it long. Sometimes I'm convinced I'm a hypochondriac or at least I bring psychosomatic illnesses upon myself just so I can be released from my strivings. Who knows? I've come to the conclusion that the answer isn't in stale introspection. It has to be outside myself.

Perfection in Love

The second formula for finding freedom is perfection in love. The perfect love John is talking about in I John 4:17–18 is, of course, God's love, not ours. If confidence were based in any way on our love, it would never be attained, for our love will always be imperfect. By perfect love, John means the perfect love God has for us. And by love being perfected, he means the love of God doing its work in freeing us from fear of punishment.

The familiar King James Version says, "fear has torment." Indeed it does. But the Revised Standard Version makes the point clearer by translating, "fear has to do with punishment." Once we know how perfectly God loves us, we are free from fear because then there is no fear that He will punish us. Love and punishment are opposite terms.

God's acceptance of us is so complete that it can only be compared to the way He regards Jesus, for John explains in I John 4:17, "As he is so are we in this world." The pronoun *he* means Jesus; "as Jesus is so are we in this world." Notice he says, "in this world"; that is, right now, not after the judgment, not after we are glorified, but right now. Before God, we are what the Bible calls "justified." This means that the sentence of the final judgment has been handed down. And the verdict is clear—we are as righteous as Jesus Christ. "There is *now* no condemnation to them which are in Christ Jesus," Romans 8:1.

The Day of Judgment

We do not have to fear Divine punishment on the day of judgment because the love of God sent Jesus to bear all the guilt of our sin. John explains in I John 4:10: "In this is love, not that we loved God, but that he loved us, and sent his son to be the expiation for our sins." God has no judgment against us. Jesus has fully repaired all the damage done to the glory of God. Sin is an enormous crime, deserving of death. But the worst part of sin is what it does to the glory of God. It is like treason against a state.

I talked with one of the judges who presided at the Eichmann trial. He explained that Israel made an exception to the law of the land and put Eichmann to death. Israel has no capital punishment. Eichmann's crime was so enormous, however, that the death penalty was re-instated. The judge said that his case involved the glory of an entire race of people. No one believes that Eichmann's death atoned for the tragic holocaust of the Jewish people in Nazi Germany. But the death of Jesus completely repaired all damage done to the glory of Heaven. Jesus was the Son of God, a Person of infinite value, and the glory He gave up on the cross was far greater than the damage done to the glory of God by human sin. The justice of God was eternally satisfied by the death of Jesus. God's grace and mercy can flow unimpeded. Thus an understanding of God's perfect love "casts out all fear." God is not against us; He is not even neutral; God is for us. And "if God be for us, who can be against us?" (Romans 8:31).

Fullness of Joy

First John 1:4 was written that "our joy may be full." Nothing brings fullness of joy like knowing the liberating love of God. This is evident in the personal testimony of a woman who found complete release from an intolerable bondage of guilt through the love of God.

The thoughts of my past were more than I could bear. I thought the only way out that I could ever find would be death. For many months I had been living in hell. Yet, I could not allow anyone else to know my feelings for fear of their hating me or their telling the whole world how horrible I had been. I was full of hate for myself, fear, shame, unworthiness, depression, etc. Although I felt this way about myself inside, I acted to others as if there was nothing wrong. Many times my husband would ask me if there was something wrong and I would always tell him "No" and try as hard as possible to change the subject. But I knew if I couldn't be completely honest with my husband, I would never be completely honest with anyone.

On Saturday night, I told him I had to talk to him and I told him exactly what I had done three years ago. I told him how much I loved him but that I would understand completely if he wanted to leave me. Instead of hating me as he very well could have, he prayed with me. Oh, how I thank God He gave me such a wonderful husband. As I told him, the weight of shame I felt was like ten thousand pounds bearing down on my body. I thought about the tremendous weight that was on our Lord when He suffered the guilt of sin for all of us. To think that He would do that for me. As we prayed, the weight was lifted . . . suddenly I was free . . . to suffer such shame and find this reality is more than words can ever describe!! I can be thankful that He has given me a worthiness. Even though in myself I am really *nothing*, through Christ I can become a real person.

PRAYER

Perfect love toward imperfect me. Lord, what kind of love is that? Love that frees from fear and covers with confidence. Love that makes living free and spontaneous. Love that makes life supernaturally natural. Lord, what a love! What a fellowship! What a joy divine. Thank You, in Christ.

Amen.

THINKING IT OVER . . .

1. Which of these words best describes you:
   condemnation?
   confidence?
2. Has the confidence of the love of God freed you from fear of punishment?
3. One of the results of knowing the perfect love of God is fullness of joy. Are you experiencing this?

Tapping in on the Laws of Life

--->>><<<---

"This is the love of God, that we keep his commandments. And his commandments are not burdensome."
                                        I John 5:3

"This is the testimony, that God gave us eternal life, and this life is in His Son."   *I John 5:11*

Building Blocks

A research project has been done by Dr. Joseph Kraut, professor of chemistry at the University of California in San Diego. He made a study of enzymes, which he terms the "building blocks of life." He says there is nothing haphazard about the way the so-called building blocks of life are put together. Given a particular function to perform, nature will devise the same machinery to do it every time. We can suppose that nature does

63

these things the same way, he says, because there is only one way to do it most efficiently. He further states that we can hypothesize that there is only one way in which living things can be assembled here or anywhere else in the universe. If the God of the atom so carefully constructed the building blocks of life, are we to imagine that man, the crown of creation, has been left to find life by mere chance? Hardly.

Love, Life, and Law

According to First John, the essence of life is living in the love of God. But the love of God is manifested to us in order that we might keep his commandments (I John 5:3). This means that the love of God enables us to tap in on the laws of life. God's commandments are God's laws. And by God's laws we mean the way life works. The commandments of God are not arbitrary rules handed down from some other world and imposed upon a foreign creation. No. The laws of God are the laws of life itself. They are a lifting up of the inner laws of reality. This is why they are "not burdensome," for they perfectly fit us. We were created by God and we work His way. So His commandments are the laws of our own inner being; they are not something strange for which we are badly made.

A Definition of Life

Biology has given us a working definition of life. Life depends upon two things: (1) an adequate environment, and (2) a correspondence with that environment. It is obvious that no organism can live without some kind of environment. Every cell must have air; every seed must have sun and soil. Take any living thing out of its environment and it dies. "Like a fish out of water" is a common proverb we all understand. An adequate environment is absolutely essential to life. And it follows that the more perfect the environment, the better are the chances for an organism to survive.

Then, too, an organism must have a correspondence with its environment. Every living thing must have a vital connection with its surroundings. An uprooted plant removed from the soil will wither at once. And here, it follows also, that the more complete the correspondence an organism has with its environment the better are the chances for life. Thus, if any living thing had a perfect environment and a complete correspondence with that environment, it would enter into life at the highest possible level.

What Is Eternal Life?

The kind of life promised in First John is called eternal life. The phrase appears six times: I John 1:2; 2:25; 3:15; 5:11; 5:13; and 5:20. Eternal life means more than living forever, for living forever could be an endless circle of boredom. Life in hell is said to be everlasting, but it hardly qualifies as eternal life. Life must have depth as well as length, and quality as well as quantity.

Eternal life implies that eternal or Divine qualities have entered into life, thus raising life to the highest possible level. This is why eternal life is synonymous with abundant life or what we might call a perfect life. Perfection, of course, means reaching a goal, not a fussy self-righteous perfection. Perhaps a better word would be completion. Eternal life is the completion of life, the realization of the "Great Upward Drive." We can understand, then, why John says, "Anyone who hates his brother is a murderer and you know that no murderer has eternal life abiding in him," (I John 3:15). The obvious conclusion is that the most significant quality of eternal life is love. Only as we learn to live in the love of God do we experience the completion of life here and now, and have the hope of a totally fulfilled, unending existence. This is eternal life.

Where Is Eternal Life?

John says, "God gave us eternal life, and this life is in his Son," (I John 5:11). Eternal life cannot be separated from Jesus Christ because He alone provides the perfect environment for the human soul. As a man, He is a perfect example, so we can "walk as he walked," (I John 2:6). And as the Son of God, He provides the power so that we can enter into life. First John 4:4 explains, "Greater is he that is in you than he that is in the world." John especially warns against the danger of drawing our life from the world. The world is defined in I John 2:15–16 as: the "lust of the flesh," probably meaning unrestrained sensual appetites; the "lust of the eyes," or materialism; and the "pride of life," or the things which center on the self. Lust differs from love in that it turns on the self, while love reaches out beyond itself to others. This suggests a necessary law of life, for anything turned in on itself lacks a correspondence with its environment and will die. To illustrate, a cancer has been called a "selfish cell." Any single cell in the human body is thought to have the capacity to become the whole body. But at a given point, it must stop its own growth and yield to a higher life beyond itself. The ways of the world are wrong because they are cancerous. They are self-centered, full of lust and hate, and this is no adequate environment for eternal life.

Correspondence with Christ

John points out the great objective of the Gospel in I John 1:3: that we "might have fellowship with the Father and with his Son Jesus Christ." Since Jesus is the perfect environment, the only thing lacking for eternal life is a correspondence with Him. The more complete our correspondence, or fellowship, is with Him, the greater will be our entrance into life. For this reason, we ought to make a declaration of dependence on Jesus.

This ought not seem strange, for the first law of all life is receptivity. No organism can give out unless it has first received. All life is derived, except the life of God. Every living thing comes from a seed, a spore, or a parent. As He began the Sermon on the Mount, Jesus explained in the first beatitude, "Blessed are the poor in spirit, for theirs is the kingdom of heaven," (Matthew 5:3). This might be paraphrased to read, "Blessed are the receptive in spirit who know they are essentially dependent beings and not self-sufficient, for then reality will back them rather than break them." We are called to have a complete correspondence with Christ, but this does not put the basis for the fellowship on the principle of works or self-effort. We learn to live in the love of God, not by struggling, but by resting and receiving.

The Law of the Parent

In natural life, there is the law of conformity to type. We might call it the law of the parent. Given a proper diet and environment, a child grows without effort. And it is only a matter of time until the child begins to take on the features of the parent. John makes a comment in I John 3:9 which is based on the strongest of biological truths, "No one born of God commits sin; for God's nature abides in him, and he cannot sin because he is born of God."

It is apparent that the word "sin" is to be taken in a special sense, for John has earlier established that all men are sinners (I John 1:8–10). It probably includes an attack on the Gnostics who claimed that only the human body could sin since it was made of matter; and it means that we will not sin in the sense of missing the ultimate goal of God for our lives. The reason we will attain eternal life and thus not "sin" is because of the law of the Parent. We are born of God; His nature abides in us. So our part is to yield to Christ and abide in Him. As Jesus said, "Consider the lilies how they grow." How do they grow? His answer, "they toil not," (Matthew 6:28). Lily-law—that is the law of our life. As the lily spontaneously and naturally gives itself up to the sun, the higher kingdom above, it grows in glorious array.

A Transformed Struggling Failure

A colleague tells how he was transformed from a "struggling failure" to a life in harmony with the ways of God. His thrilling testimony makes an apt summary for this series:

I have always been small framed and until recently very skinny. I envied my male peers who had fine physiques and I felt inferior and at times even "feminine" because of my size. I wore heavy undershirts because I felt they made me look bigger in the shoulders. I couldn't begin to add up the amount of money I spent on "weight-on" tablets and liquids. I did everything I could to put on weight, but in the process of trying I was a nervous wreck; consequently, I lost instead of gaining weight.

It is a slow and painful process to grow up and face the reality of this world. In looking at myself, I have had to learn that I am nothing—that in me dwells no good thing. I have had to learn that life isn't about to track me down and beg me to enter its gates. No, life doesn't hunt the individual but it moves on; and in its wake I can find the majority of men groping in their own small ego-centric world, floundering and crying for help because life didn't bow down and kiss the ground in front of them. I know because I was there, cursing this world because it didn't revolve around me and my needs.

When I graduated from High School in 1966, I was a very deeply disturbed, confused, and immature "child." I was not living in accordance with the laws of God and life wasn't in my favor. I was going against the grain of life. I hated God, my parents, my friends, and life itself—I was very bitter. I left home and took up residence in another state. It was only through a "death-bed" experience that I had a personal encounter with Jesus Christ. Just because I accepted Christ didn't mean that all of life would switch to meet me but it did mean that I immediately switched and instead of going against life I began to go with life. But the Old Nature wasn't going down without a fight and thus a long road of knocks and trouble was to follow.

This rough road was the result of this great truth that, at that time, I didn't know—Life doesn't reverse its course according to the individual, but *the individual enters the flow of life by complying to those laws of life* that God has woven into the structure of living in this world. I was still a struggling failure. I was ego-centered, proud, and boastful. But now as I sit here penning my thoughts I realize that I am a changed individual; where once there was anguish, despair, self-works, pride, etc., there is now the peace and satisfaction of God. What is the key? The key that I have realized is a yielding to life through Jesus Christ and conforming to the teaching that He has laid down. [*He closes with a prayer.*] "Oh, God, let me be humble so You may use me the way *YOU* want to, and not the way *I* want You to use me."

PRAYER

Lord, do You mean that You designed all the universe to bring life to me? And You sent Jesus to show me what real life is? And You gave Jesus to usher me in to this eternal life? Lord, I give up; I want to submit completely to a sovereign like You.

Amen.

THINKING IT OVER . . .

1. Do you feel that God's commandments are arbitrary rules imposed on you?
2. How are God's laws designed so that they will not be burdensome to you?
3. The author states: "Life depends upon two things: (1) an adequate environment, and (2) a correspondence with that environment." How does God provide both of these so that you can have abundant life? Can this become a part of your life?